A Note to Parents

For many children, learning math is difficult and "I hate math!" is their first response—to which many parents silently add "Me, too!" Children often see adults comfortably reading and writing, but they rarely have such models for mathematics. And math fear can be catching!

The easy-to-read stories in this *Hello, Math Reader* series were written to give children a positive introduction to mathematics, and parents a pleasurable re-acquaintance with a subject that is important to everyone's life. *Hello Math* stories make mathematical ideas accessible, interesting, and fun for children. The activities and suggestions at the end of each book provide parents with a hands-on approach to help children develop mathematical interest and confidence.

Enjoy the mathematics!
• Give your child a chance to retell the story. The more familiar children are with the story, the more they will understand its mathematical concepts.
• Use the colorful illustrations to help children "hear and see" the math at work in the story.
• Treat the math activities as games to be played for fun. Follow your child's lead. Spend time on those activities that engage your child's interest and curiosity.
• Activities, especially ones using physical materials, help make abstract mathematical ideas concrete.

Learning is a messy process. Learning about math calls for children to become immersed in lively experiences that help them make sense of mathematical concepts and symbols.

Although learning about numbers is basic to math, other ideas, such as identifying shapes and patterns, measuring, collecting and interpreting data, reasoning logically, and thinking about chance, are also important. By reading these stories and having fun with the activities, you will help your child enthusiastically say "*Hello, Math*," instead of "I hate math."

—Marilyn Burns
National Mathematics Educator
Author of *The I Hate Mathematics! Book*

ISBN 0-590-67360-2

Text and art copyright © 1996 by Scholastic Inc.
The activities on pages 25-32 copyright © 1996 by Marilyn Burns.
All rights reserved. Published by Scholastic Inc.
CARTWHEEL BOOKS and the CARTWHEEL BOOKS logo
are registered trademarks of Scholastic Inc.
HELLO MATH READER and the HELLO MATH READER logo
are trademarks of Scholastic Inc.

Library of Congress Cataloging-in-Publication Data

Burns, Marilyn, 1941-
    How many feet? How many tails? / story and activities by Marilyn
Burns; illustrated by Lynn Adams.
        p.   cm. — (Hello math reader. Level 2)
    Summary: As two children take a walk with their grandfather, they use their counting skills to help answer a series of animal riddles. Includes related activities.
    ISBN 0-590-67360-2
    [1. Counting — Fiction. 2. Riddles — Fiction. 3. Animals — Fiction.]
    I. Adams, Lynn (Lynn Joan), ill. II. Title. III. Series.
PZ7.B93739Ho   1996
[E] — dc20   96-7970
                                                                      CIP
                                                                       AC

20 19 18 17 16 15 14   2 3 4 5 6/0

Printed in the U.S.A.   23

First Scholastic printing, September 1996

How Many Feet? How Many Tails?

A Book of Math Riddles

Story and Math Activities by Marilyn Burns
Illustrated by Lynn Adams

Hello Math Reader — Level 2

SCHOLASTIC INC.
New York Toronto London Auckland Sydney

We went for a walk
with Grandpa.
He likes riddles.
So do we.

What has eight feet,
two tails,
and pulls a wagon?

Two horses.

What has twelve feet,
three tails,
and sits in a
window?

Three bunnies.

What has zero feet,
three tails,
and lives in a bowl?

Three fish.

What has ten feet,
five tails,
and walks in the park?

One mama duck and
four ducklings.

What has six feet,
three tails,
and eats in a tree?

One papa bird and
two baby birds.

What has one tail,
zero legs,
and hides in the grass?

One snake.

What has four feet,
two tails,
and floats on the pond?

Two swans.

What has twelve feet,
three tails,
and sleeps under the porch?

One mother cat and
two kittens.

What has four feet,
one tail,
and lives in a little house?

One dog.

What has ten feet,
zero tails,
and lives in the big house?

We do!

• About the Activities •

Children love riddles. Even when they know the answers to riddles, children delight in hearing them over and over again. The story and activities in this book use children's interest in riddles to give them practice with counting, and help build their understanding of numerical relationships.

For children, learning to count is a first step in learning to make sense of numbers. Typically, young children learn to say the numbers in order — one, two, three, and so on — before they learn to count objects one by one or associate each number name with a specific quantity. It's only after many counting experiences that children develop understanding of numbers and learn to use numbers to solve problems.

Children can solve all of the number riddles in the story by searching the illustrations and counting. The visual clues give children experience with seeing numerical quantities in real-world contexts. The pictures also help children become more flexible in using numbers by showing them how numbers relate to one another. The answer to each riddle is provided, so children only have to turn the page to find the solution or confirm their counting.

The activity directions are written for you to read along with your child. Children may enjoy doing their favorite riddle activities again and again. Encourage them to do so. Or try a different activity at each reading. Be open to your child's interests, and have fun with math!

— Marilyn Burns

You'll find tips and suggestions for guiding the activities whenever you see a box like this!

Retelling the Story

At the beginning of the story, Grandpa saw two horses pulling a wagon. He counted eight feet and two tails. Count the horses' feet and tails to see if you get the same numbers as Grandpa did.

Next, the girl saw three bunnies in a store window. Count to find out if you see twelve feet and three tails.

The boy saw three fish in a fishbowl. Count to be sure there are zero feet and three tails.

Count through the rest of the book to check the number of feet and tails on each page.

In Your House

How many feet and tails will sleep at your house tonight? Make a guess. Then draw a picture and count to check.

When the boy in the story tells the riddle about the snake, he uses the word "zero." This may be a new word for your child, but using it in context is the best way for your child to become familiar and comfortable with it. You might want to play a game with your child: What do we have zero of in our house? Playing this game many times will help your child learn the meaning of zero.

Toy Count

How many feet and tails does each of your toys have?

Your child will most likely reach for toys that have feet or tails — stuffed animals, toy soldiers, dolls, and so on. Asking them about toys that don't have any feet or tails — balls, cars, trucks, and so on — gives you a way to reinforce the idea of zero.

Toy Riddle Game

Play this riddle game with another person.

Think about two of your toys. Tell the other person how many feet and tails your two toys have altogether.

Now the other person guesses which toys you are thinking about. (The person guessing may pick the wrong toys, but they may have the same number of feet and tails as in your riddle! How can this happen?)

Take turns so you each have a chance to guess.

Two by Two

One person has two feet.
Two people have four feet.
Three people have six feet.
How many feet do four people have?
How many do five people have?

The number of feet goes up by twos. Try counting by twos — 2, 4, 6, 8, and so on.

If your child hasn't learned to count by twos, using concrete objects can help. Line up pairs of shoes and count by twos with your child. Or take out pennies or buttons, arrange them in twos, and count. Experiences such as these are useful not only for helping your child to learn to count by twos, but also for seeing how this sequence relates to a regular pattern.

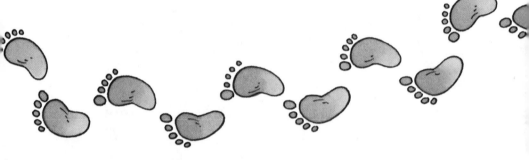

A Two by Two Riddle

If there were 10 people on a bus, how many feet would there be? What if more people got on the bus? Pick a number, and then figure out how many feet that number of people would have.

Grandpa's Riddle

Grandpa said he grew up in a house where there were 12 feet and one tail. Who could have lived with Grandpa? How many different answers can you think of?